The Minnesota Gardener

How to get the most out of your Minnesota garden while taking the least out of your time and pocket.

The short months of a Minnesota summer

are precious,

get the most out of them.

About the Author

*Nancy Ann comes from a long line of green thumbs.
It all began when her great-grandfather came over
from Germany and started up the family greenhouse
business in Golden Valley, MN.*

A business that employed many family members

– four generations deep.

Nancy Ann has been gardening ever since

she was a little sprout.

Happy Gardening!

Nancy Ann

The Minnesota Gardener

A quick guide to getting the most out of your Minnesota garden while taking the least out of your time and pocket.

By Nancy Ann

2017 Edition

This book is dedicated to the two green thumbs in my life, my father and my grandfather.

Table of Contents

Introduction

As a Minnesota gardener, you know the importance of getting your crops and flowers planted on time in order to allow them to grow to maturity. Whether you are an avid gardener or just starting out, this book will provide you with simple and inexpensive steps that you can take all year round to make your Minnesota garden flourish. It is designed to be a quick read that will provide you with important tips that will improve your gardening experience while increasing your yield.

No matter your passion — flowers, vegetables, or both; the same techniques can be applied in order to reward you with bountiful blooms or harvest.

By following simple steps from month to month you will accomplish a lot without overburdening your free time and your pocketbook.

You can create a colorful backyard retreat full of flowers, butterflies, and hummingbirds that you will love to come home to after a long day at work.

Enjoy the satisfaction of self-reliance and independence that you will feel when you grow and preserve enough food to feed your family throughout the entire year. Fresh food that tastes better and that you put up for storage without using chemicals or preservatives.

If you sell your produce, you will be able to provide your customers with the highest quality of stock that they will come back for time and time again.

By planning ahead, taking notes, and applying these time and money saving guidelines, you will be able to enjoy your garden without feeling overwhelmed.

Instead of trying to do everything in three or four months, you are spreading the tasks out over a twelve-month period which will give you more time sitting in an Adirondack chair overlooking your beautiful garden rather than hunched over in a row weeding it.

Throughout this book, you will find space to take notes, some quick reference guides, and a page dedicated to your wish list. Feel free to highlight and add your own notes throughout.

Get started today!

Note: The average highs and lows cited in this book are based on Minneapolis, MN temperatures.

January

Average MN High: 24° F

Average MN Low: 8° F

It's January in Minnesota. The holidays have come and gone. You notice that the days are just a bit longer. Seed catalogs begin to arrive in the mail and you catch yourself staring at your garden from your kitchen window. Sure, the ground is frozen and covered with snow, but in your mind, you're envisioning lush green plants, hummingbirds, and butterflies.

Snap out of it! There is much to do right now other than daydreaming! Save those pleasant thoughts for when you lay your head on your pillow at night. Don't let the frozen tundra of Zone 4 fool you into thinking that you have to wait until you see the first Robin of Spring in order to start your garden.

Au contraire, there are many things that you can be doing for the upcoming gardening season. Minnesota has a warm crop gardening window of three months, four, if you're lucky. By being organized and working along with Mother Nature, you can extend your gardening season and increase the amount of your harvest.

Mapping Out Your Garden

Whether you have a single, large garden bed or several different beds throughout your property, you will need to map out your planting areas. Begin by drawing each bed to scale. This can be done in a spiral notebook—no need to get fancy. If you don't know the sizes of your beds, then bundle up, go outside, and measure them. You'll only need to do this once and then you'll have this worthwhile information for years to follow. If you find yourself extending your gardening area, then be sure to update your notes.

Once you have your garden spaces measured and scaled drawings sketched into your notebook, you can begin to plan out your garden.

> *GREEN THUMB TIP:* It's handy to get a multi-subject spiral-bound notebook in which you can keep all of your gardening notes year after year. You will be glad that you have data from the previous years to refer to and it will help you plan for future years.

Start by understanding the sun. Note how and when it shines on your planting area. If you've never paid attention to this previously, observe it during the upcoming year and take notes in your garden notebook. This is valuable information.

Right now, in January, the sun is low in the

sky and its path will be very different than it will be in July. There are many things to consider when it comes to the effect that the sunlight has on your garden. Most plants that produce food need at least 6-8 hours of sunlight each day. Buildings, fences, and trees can cast shadows over your planting space, thus robbing it of beneficial sunlight. Be sure to look at your neighbors' trees, too. The shadow of a tall maple knows no boundaries! Not all shade is bad. For example, in the middle of a hot July day, the cooling relief of an hour or two in the freckled shade of a tree may be welcomed by your beans.

Determine What to Plant

Now that you have measured out your planting space and figured out, at least somewhat, the path of the sun and how it will shine and cast shadows, you can begin to make your list of what you're going to plant. Unless you're just putting in a row of beans and a couple of tomato plants, it is very helpful to write out a list of everything that you wish to plant. Leave a couple of blank lines between each item on your list so that you can add notes about them. Information on spacing between plants, the height of the plant, and beneficial planting companions, etc…will prove to be useful. Knowing and planning ahead of time will help to ensure a more successful harvest. It would be a shame to plant your fast-growing beans next to your slower, yet taller, growing tomatoes only to find out too late that, come July, the path of the sun causes the tomatoes to shadow your beans.

If you are new to gardening or just haven't had good luck with it, take the time to do this planning on paper. Most of it you will need to do only once. Over the following years, you can simply refer to your notes.

The landscape of every yard and garden is different, so by taking good notes you are getting to know your own little ecosystem on a very personal level. If you are planting only vegetables, it's wise to include early flowering plants that will attract bees, hummingbirds, and other pollinators to your garden.

Now that you have your list, along with the characteristics and requirements of each plant, you can begin to plot out your garden.

> *GREEN THUMB TIP:* Do this step with a pencil and have an eraser handy!

If you are planting in last year's garden bed, the first thing you should consider is rotating your crop. Tomatoes, for example, should not be planted in the same space more than two years in a row. This will mean that over the years you will be coming up with a few different garden plots for the same space. You will learn, too, what works and what doesn't. Take good notes!

It's important that you allow for proper spacing. Proper spacing allows plants to reach their full size and also permits good air circulation. While it may seem like you could plant your beans three inches apart instead of four inches apart, you will likely end up with inferior plants. It's better to have a row of 10 well-producing plants than a row of 15 mediocre plants.

Your spacing between the rows is equally as important. You want enough room to work without damaging the row behind you. If space is an issue, look into different varieties. Maybe instead of bush beans, pole beans are your answer. Just remember to plant with the path of the sun in mind.

Once you have your garden mapped out, you will have a good idea as to how many seeds you will need, how many garden markers to make or buy, and if you are going the route of transplants for some veggies, you'll have all that information at your fingertips, too. Now you can buy your seed starting supplies, or wash up last years, and get ready for planting!

February

Average MN High: 29° F

Average MN Low: 13° F

For the Zone 4 Minnesotan gardener, there are several flowers and vegetables that need to be started indoors anywhere from four to eight weeks before the last frost. (The last frost in Minnesota is approximately May 1st.) The rule of thumb is to begin direct sowing in your garden by May 31st. By starting seeds early, you extend your growing season. Benefits of this include the fact that you will be enjoying things like fresh tomatoes earlier and battling an early frost is of less concern.

Getting a Head Start on the Season

If you have a nice sunny window where you can set up a table (covered with plastic and then newspaper) to start planting a few seeds, you can get a great head start on your planting season. While February may seem a bit early, there are many things that you can start. Tomatoes are a great thing to start now. All of the large transplants that you buy at the garden centers are being started at this time of year. Just realize that tomatoes require to be transplanted several times, and each time they are moved into a pot that is at least an inch larger than the last, so you need to make sure that your table and sunny window can accommodate. You may opt to start with only two or three tomatoes at this point and start more in March or April when it begins to warm up.

Other things to start are your herbs, which if they're annuals, such as basil, you may just want to grow in a pot, anyway. Broccoli, cauliflower, and peppers can also be started in February. Plant enough that will exceed your garden plan should some of your seeds not sprout or seedlings not make it. Wait until April for planting squash, cucumbers, and watermelons; these plants grow quickly and are very large.

Grow Lights and Heat Mats

Grow lights are something that you should consider purchasing. Your seedlings will naturally reach and grow toward the window and even if you turn the tray several times a day, they will eventually become leggy. Using grow lights directly above your seeding tray will greatly reduce the reaching and stretching. Instead of tall and skinny, your plants will be stout and sturdy. Provide your seedlings with at least 10 hours of light.

If you don't have an ideal window, you can still create a good growing environment—even in a basement! (Grow lights are a must in a basement environment.) Soil temperature is just as important as light for starting seeds. Most garden centers carry heat mats made specifically for seeding. One or two of these would be a good investment and should be used, especially if you are set up in a basement. Most seeds require warmth in order to germinate properly. A shallow seeding tray filled with peat or seeding soil equipped with a clear dome lid on a heat mat creates an ideal environment for germination.

One day prior to planting your seeds, moisten the soil thoroughly; not too wet and not too dry. Then put your dome over your tray and let the soil heat up on the heat mat. You will see moisture build up on the dome, this condensation is normal.

GREEN THUMB TIP: Before lifting the dome off of your tray, flick it with your finger so that the droplets fall back down onto the soil. This will put some moisture back into the soil and prevent a drippy mess.

Also, get a general-purpose spray bottle for misting your seeds. This water should be kept at room temperature. As your seeds sprout and are well rooted, you can use a spouted bottle for delivering more water to your plants. A well-washed mustard bottle works great for this task. Keep your water container on the heat mat, if there is room, or on your table in the sun. When it runs low, be sure to fill it so it gets back to room temperature before the next watering.

Plant your seeds to the depth provided on the packet in which they came. If you are planting seeds from a generous neighbor, you can use the old-school rule of planting twice as deep as the seed is large. Using a sharpened pencil to make a hole for your seed is ideal.

Variety of tomatoes started in February indoors under a grow light.

GREEN THUMB TIP: Plug your grow lights into a timer so your plants get the appropriate amount of light and darkness without the concern of forgetting to them on and off manually.

When you plant, be sure to mark your trays and pots. Do this as soon as you plant to avoid forgetting dates and mislabeling. Include on the marker the type of plant, the date you planted, and the germination period. These are also good things to record in your garden notebook.

If you have a heated sunroom or greenhouse, take advantage and really give your garden a start! Refer to your garden map and plant more than enough to allow for bad seeds and weak plants.

However, don't plant so much that your efforts and seeds go to waste.

No matter where you set up shop, coddle and treat your nursery gently. Be patient. Your seeds are about to perform a natural wonder. Some will sprout before the germination period, and some after; and some, perhaps not at all. After one or two weeks beyond the germination period, you can feel comfortable in dropping another seed in the failed seed's place. This way the plant will only be a little behind the others.

March

Average MN High: 41° F

Average MN Low: 24° F

March is a teaser month. Some years, Minnesota is still knee deep in snow! Other years, there are days that are just so warm that you feel like you could be planting directly into your garden. You find that you are able to work up the soil and the probability of winter returning seems impossible. Avoid the temptation to believe that this year summer will come early. Even if that may end up being the case, trust in the May 31st planting date.

Sure, some years you can play around with it by a week or two, but it's best to start your direct seeding and transplanting according to this standard target date. It takes only one cold night to undo all of the time and effort from the past several weeks. If this happens you will find yourself in one of three situations:

1. Starting over, which, at this point, you will have a late start.
2. Buying transplants, a more expensive route and of limited variety.
3. Empty handed.

So, what can you do in March? Plenty!

23

Marching Forward

You can begin by giving your plants a workout. Start off slowly. The first step is to turn off your heat mat during the day. By now your plants should be strong enough to manage without it. Remove the plastic lid, if you haven't already. Your plants should not touch the top of the lid. If the outside temperature is a warm 50 degrees, open the window that they are in front of just a crack and let a gentle breeze blow through them. This will help strengthen your plants. Do this in ½ hour to an hour increments, closing the window for an equal amount of time, then open it again. It's also a good idea to turn your plants so that they are not always being blown the same direction. Keep the window closed once the warm 50 degrees has passed for the day and turn your heating mat back on at night. Each day your plants will adapt just a bit more to what nature has in store for them.

After a week or two of the indoor exercise, you can begin to give your young plants some real, live outdoor time. As warmer days become more frequent and your plants become stronger and accustomed to the fluctuation in temperature, you can start setting the whole flat outside. Do not set it on your cement patio slab, but rather keep it several feet off the ground. The top of a black BBQ grill can be ideal for this as it absorbs heat from the sun and will help keep the soil at a desirable temperature.

It's important to know the actual temperature. While it may feel nice and warm to you, it may be a bit too chilly for your seedlings. Remember, they have been pampered

with a warm seeding bed and heated house. But if you find that you have a warm 50 degree day with barely a breeze, find a protected nook in the sun and give your plants some outdoor time. While you do want your plants to become accustomed to natures elements, you also want to keep them protected from strong March breezes. As the next few weeks go by, your plants will become stronger and stronger.

Monitor the moisture in the soil, as it will dry out more quickly than when you had your plants contained under their dome and in the house. The surface of the soil is most certain to appear dry, this is okay as long as the roots have moist soil below.

Should you find that March doesn't offer the appropriate conditions for exercising your plants, then by all means, don't do it! You can still turn off the heating mat and put a fan somewhere that will simulate a gentle breeze. Use an oscillating fan and move it around every now and then so that you are creating a random, soft breeze, as would Mother Nature.

Remember to keep notes of dates, temperatures, and the status of your plants.

You will be so glad that you did! Why, I even know people that take pictures of their plants at various stages! Joking aside, I have found this to be a very helpful tool. If you do take pictures, make sure that you have the date feature activated on your camera.

By March you may also find that it is necessary to pinch back some of your plants. Tomatoes and herbs benefit especially from being pinched back. You will get stronger and bushier plants.

These are my tomatoes that I started in February. This photo was taken March 13th after transplanting them. I started them indoors under a grow light and moved them out to my little greenhouse which I keep heated with a small, oil filled, electric space heater. I set the little greenhouse up inside my larger 14' x 14' hoophouse.

If you started your seeds in plain peat moss, it's probably time to give them some food. The root system of your seedlings should now be strong enough to fertilize. If you buy fertilizer from the store, at this point use a liquid fertilizer mixed at half the recommended strength. Otherwise, you can make your own compost tea. Feed your young plants every third watering. As with your plant water, your fertilized mixture should be at room temperature when applied. Provide support for your growing seedlings as necessary.

If, at this point, the snow is gone and the ground has begun to thaw, go ahead and start to work the soil in your garden. It doesn't matter if it snows again, as you won't be planting yet. But you will be that much farther ahead! Leave a two-foot by two-foot square of undisturbed soil so that you can monitor the soil temperature. You can work this area up later. The reason for this is because once you work the soil, it will warm up more quickly on the surface but just below it there could still be frost. You want the most realistic and accurate reading.

Begin to take and record the soil temperature. You can find soil thermometers at most nursery supply stores. These thermometers are encased in a metal guard to protect the glass from breaking. Try to find one that is at least six inches long, eight inches is even better. Insert the thermometer into unworked soil that has been resting all winter. If the ground is thawed, it should slide in with relative ease.

Don't force it or it may break. You will just have to wait until the ground has had more exposure to the warmer temperatures. Leave your thermometer in the ground, undisturbed, for one hour. Pull the thermometer from the ground and record the temperature in your notebook immediately. Be sure to write the date, time, and location within your garden along with the air and soil temperatures. Continue to monitor and record this data, using a fresh spot for your thermometer each time. (Don't use the same hole twice.) The overnight temperature of the ground should be 60 degrees consistently before you begin to direct sow or transplant warm weather crops.

April

Average MN High: 58° F

Average MN Low: 37° F

    Your urge to plant is probably taunting you, but still hold off on those warm crop veggies. Your patience will be rewarded. The good news is that there are some things that you can begin to plant four weeks before the last frost, which, in much of Minnesota is around May 1st. Also, April is a very busy preparation month and you will find that there is much to do that will keep your mind and hands occupied.

Lay Out Your Soaker Hoses

    If you use soaker hoses throughout your garden, the beginning of April is a good time to get them straightened out. Take the time on a warm, sunny day to uncoil them and let them lay flat until they are much more manageable. This will make it easier to find and repair any "leaks" that they may have developed. Leaks which will erode holes in your garden and make the rest of the hose much less effective.

    After you have them laid out on your lawn or driveway, hook them up to the faucet. While the water is on, tie a string around the hose where you find any large sprays of water. This will mark your leak. An easy and effective fix for these types of leaks is the ever-versatile duct tape. Turn off the water and allow the hose to dry thoroughly. Wrap duct tape tightly around the leaky spot that you marked with your string, which you now may remove.

Once the curls have been worked out of the hoses and any leaks have been repair, you can carefully weave them through your garden using your garden design map as your guide. (Provided you have already worked up the soil.) Anchor your hose here and there with landscaping staples to keep the general lay out, yet allow enough wiggle room to adjust when you actually plant and transplant. You will anchor them firmly later as you plant.

> *GREEN THUMB TIP:* If you have a closet full of old wire hangers that you don't use, cut the shoulders off of them and use those as your anchors.

Rain Barrels

If you have a rain barrel, good for you! This is a great way to collect and store water that plants love. City water has been treated with chemicals that your plants do not need.

Find a place for your rain barrel where it will be easily accessible for your gardening needs. Even a small shed outfitted with a gutter system is sufficient to fill your barrel after a nice rainfall. I keep mine on an elevated corner off of the garage and attach a 15-foot hose to the spigot on the bottom of the barrel. (This was a cheap hose that sprung a leak so I just cut it off and discarded the rest.) When I water my garden or potted plants, I use my rain water first. It's great for house plants, too!

Every now and then, especially before a rain, I drain the entire barrel so it can fill up again with fresh rain water. It's important to keep your rain barrel clean and fresh as possible. If you do not have a rain barrel, put it on your wish list and keep your eye out for a bargain!

Cool Weather Crops

After taking the soil temperature (again!) and it (the soil) has been consistently 45-50 degrees Fahrenheit overnight, refer to your garden map and begin direct sowing vegetables such as carrots, beets, onions, radishes, lettuce, spinach, and potatoes. Be sure to mark your rows well so that it is obvious where you planted. Anchor your soaker hoses firmly along your rows as you plant. Keep the soaker hose 3-4 inches away from your seed row. Water gently after planting, either by hand or soaker hoses.

GREEN THUMB TIP: Consider planting only a portion of your radish seeds, then plant some more the following week, then again, the week after that. Most varieties take only 21 days, so you can get several plantings in before the soil becomes too warm. You can also apply this practice to your lettuce and spinach.

Cucumbers, Squash, and Melons

April is a good time to start your cucumbers, squash, and melons indoors. There are several reasons to wait to plant these in April as opposed to February. They are large and fast growing plants. They will take over your home if you plant too early. (I learned this the hard way!) They should be transplanted, carefully, and only once. You'll want to transplant from the pot that you started them in directly into their final spot in the garden. If planted too early, they will flower before the bees and other pollinating insects are available; although you can hand-pollinate them yourself. Waiting until April for these types of plants will still give you a head start, yet you will find them much more manageable within your home and at transplanting time.

During the first two weeks of April, do a final transplanting that is needed prior to putting your plants into your garden at the end of May. Transplanting may seem relatively easy, but to the plants it can be stressful if not done with care. Each time you uproot a plant, it needs to re-establish its home, and time must be given for the plant to do so, which is at least two weeks.

Depending upon the temperature, begin to harden off your plants. Slowly acclimating them to the natural elements of the outdoors will go a long way in preventing transplant shock. As each day becomes longer and the temperature rises, you can

extend the amount of time that you expose your plants. Stay vigilant of their soil moisture, strong breezes or winds, and adverse weather. They will welcome a nice, misty spring rain provided it's not too cool out, but heavier rains, certainly downpours, should be avoided. Hardening off your plants is an important step, but it will not happen overnight.

On the other end of the spectrum, seeding trays and pots readily absorb the sun's heat and because they hold only a small amount of soil, they will dry out quickly. This will cause your plants to wilt, which can weaken or even kill them. You do not want to set them out and leave for work for the day. Even if the weather cooperates, squirrels and rabbits will sniff out their tender roots and eat them.

You could purchase a small greenhouse constructed from aluminum poles, PVC connections, and a thin, plastic covering, or even make your own, and move your plants into it instead of bringing them in and out every day. These are great, but they cannot be left to their own devices.

These are the same tomatoes on April 13ᵗʰ.

When putting it up, be sure to secure it to the ground, as you would a tent. Strong winds can blow it over or twist the framing. When it rains, the roof will pool up and you will find that it needs to be dumped, sometimes repeatedly during a single rainfall.

A greenhouse does not automatically make your plants grow. You need to monitor the temperature, soil moisture, and air circulation. During a sunny spring day, while it may be only 40 or 50 degrees outside, your greenhouse temperature may soar above 90 degrees. These high temps will dry out the soil and wilt your plants. Try to find one that has a door on both ends, this feature helps a lot with ventilation. Most come with shelving, which is great for keeping your young plants up off of the cooler ground.

You will want to continue to monitor (and record) the overnight temps. Unless you heat your little greenhouse, April temperatures can drop below freezing. Hanging a thermometer that tracks the high and low temps for the day is very handy. Hang it at the same level as your plants, not your eye level, as heat rises.

As long as you keep a good eye on things, these mini-greenhouses are a relatively inexpensive way to help your plants along. When assembled and taken down carefully each season, they will last a long time.

GREEN THUMB TIP: Be sure to save the directions that come with your greenhouse and take the time to mark each part with a *Sharpie*. (Yes, another life lesson learned!)

While each year is its own and the temperature can range vastly from year to year in Minnesota, you will find that keeping temperature records to be a very useful resource for you.

May

Average MN High: 69° F

Average MN Low: 49° F

The month you've been waiting for is finally here! Take a moment to look back at all of the busy preparation work you have done the past four months. You should have a feeling of satisfaction and gladness that you did not wait until May to try to squeeze all of that work into one month. Transplanting and direct sowing are just around the corner and you are well prepared for it!

Prior to transplanting at the end of the month, continue to monitor your soil temperature. Start leaving your thermometer in the earth overnight and check it early in the morning before the sun hits it. Do this for several nights during the first weeks of May. This will give you a good idea of what the temperature the roots of your plants will be subjected to during the night. If you've churned up your two foot by two foot section where you had been taking the temperature, then stick it in a nearby area where it won't get stepped on but where the reading would be relative to your garden area.

If the overnight air temps allow you to leave your plants out all night, then do so. It's time to cut the apron strings!

37

Place your plants in the approximate location of where they will be transplanted at the end of the month. This will help them adjust to the sun and shadows of their final home. It will be one less thing that your plant has to adapt to during transplanting. Continue to be mindful of any possible frost warnings and provide protection/coverage for your seedlings if necessary. Better safe than sorry!

While you patiently continue to wait until the end of May, busy yourself with all of the prep work that needs to be done. If you are putting in beans, you will need to protect them before they emerge. Rabbits will nip them off as soon as the first true leaves appear. To combat this, get a roll of one inch mesh chicken wire that is 18 to 24 inches in height. Roll it out on your yard, measure out and cut strips that will extend six inches beyond each end of your garden row. Then cut the strip in half the long way, thus giving you two long strips. (This is another task that you will need to do only once as you can save these row covers year after year.) Fold the strips in half in order to make a long "tent" that will cover your row. Make as many of these row covers as you will need. Set your row covers aside until planting time.

Make a checklist of last minute things you'll need come planting day, i.e., garden markers, landscape staples, tomato cages, etc…You don't want to have to run to the garden supply store once you begin planting. Having everything you need ready and waiting will allow you to put your garden in more efficiently and with relative ease.

If Mother Nature allows and you are confident in the weather forecast, you can begin to put your garden in during the last week of May. Start with the plants that you will be direct sowing, such as beans. The reason for this is because it will be easier for you to be on your hands and knees without having to worry about knocking over or stepping on your transplants. It's a good idea to set your transplants aside and out of the way while you are direct sowing.

As you complete each row, anchor down your soaker hose with landscape staples or your homemade anchors. Then cover your row with your chicken wire tent and anchor it down. Pinch the open ends of your tents in order to keep rabbits and squirrels from entering. Fill out your row marker with helpful planting data such as plant type, date planted, and days to maturity. When you've completed a row, move on to the next. By completing all of the steps for each row instead of planting all of them, then going back to secure the soaker hose, then securing the tents, then marking them, is a better way to do it. For one thing, your completed row is now obvious to you and others. Even your dog won't step on it. It also allows you a stopping point. With all the steps completed, you can stop planting for a couple of hours or a day without any worries. Once all of your direct sowing is completed, it's time to transplant! First, determine if it is a

good day to transplant. You want your plants to go through the least amount of stress and to avoid transplant shock. Mid-morning is a good time to transfer your plants into their new home. The day is just beginning to warm up and yet the hot sun won't be beating down upon them. Avoid transplanting on hot, cloudless days.

Review your garden map and determine which row you are going to put in first. Take your transplants, peppers for example, and set each potted plant in the spot where it is to be planted. Lay out the entire row. Starting at one end, dig a hole deep enough so that your plant will be buried up to the soil line.

> *GREEN THUMB TIP:* Set your plant, while still in the pot, into the hole to measure and gauge its depth and size.

If you are opting to fertilize at this point, dig the hole a bit deeper, sprinkle in your fertilizer, and then cover it with a 1" layer of soil so that the fertilizer doesn't burn the roots of your transplant. Make the hole wide enough so that when you backfill it, the roots can easily expand to the softened soil. Gently remove your transplant from its pot, gently tease out the roots a little bit, and set it in the hole.

The soil line of the hole and your plant should be about the same.

GREEN THUMB TIP: Tomatoes can be planted deeper, up to their first leaves. If you look closely at the stem of a tomato plant, you'll see little hairs on it. These little hairs will form into roots and make your plant even stronger.

It's fine to loosen the roots from the root ball, but try to leave the bulk of the potting soil intact and place it in the hole. Backfill the rest of the space evenly around your transplant gently. Pat the dirt in firmly. You don't want to pack the soil so tight that it damages the roots or that it is so compressed that the plant won't readily spread its roots outward toward new soil.

Even if your transplants don't require support at this time, now is a good time to pound in stakes and set cages around them. It's much easier when they are small and out of the way. If you're using stakes, be sure to put in some that will be tall enough to accommodate the plant at maturity. If you can, at least put one tie on the plant to give it support from wind and downpours. Short bamboo stakes work well for this. Tie loosely enough to allow wiggle room and growth.

After transplanting, water each plant gently. If your transplants appear wilted and defeated the first few days, be patient as they will likely spring back to vibrant, healthy plants.

June

Average MN High: 79° F

Average MN Low: 59° F

As you step back and look at your garden at this point, it's like looking at braces on somebody's teeth with all of the supports and chicken wire. But, like with braces, it will be beautiful in the end.

You may feel at this point that all of your work is done and now you can kick back and relax as your garden grows. This is true, if you don't mind weeds, broken stems, and inferior results. But if you're serious about harvesting your best crop, June has its share of work.

Keeping the Weeds Back

The one thing you should do for certain is stay on weed control. This is a manual task. Weeds will compete against your vegetables for the moisture and nutrients, and usually win if given the chance. Anything you spray on your garden will be absorbed in some manner by the foods that you are growing for you and your family to consume. Think twice before applying chemicals. Research them to better educate yourself.

Weeding is as big of a job as your garden is large, however there are many natural and non-invasive ways to stay ahead of the weeds. If you use soaker hoses, you're already one step ahead. If you didn't lay down soaker hoses and have now decided to, now is the time to put them in, but it will need to be done with utmost care. Trying to weave and anchor your hoses among larger plants later is difficult and will result in damaging many plants.

Use landscape cloth in your rows between plants. Make sure, though, that it has not been treated with chemicals to prevent weed growth. A quality, professional grade of black or gray landscape cloth is worth buying. You can simply roll it out to the length of your row and cut it. Then, depending upon the width you need, cut the length into strips. Anchor them with landscape staples. In many instances, you can use the same staples that are used for your hoses and/or chicken wire tents. Viola! You have just eliminated A LOT of weeding. You will enjoy having your rows covered with the cloth as you walk through your garden, especially after a rain.

> *GREEN THUMB TIP:* Professional grade landscape fabric can be cleaned off and dried thoroughly at the end of the season and used the following year. The staples can be reused, as well.

Straw also makes a good row cover. (Both straw and cloth will help your garden retain moisture.) Straw is not as neat as the cut and lay approach that landscape cloth, but its golden color looks very nice among the green plants. Some weeds will make it through your straw barrier, but they are easily managed if you take the time to walk up and down your garden rows each day and pull any that you see. You can throw your weeds into your compost if there are no seed heads on them, which can come back to haunt you the following year.

With straw, you will find that any oat seeds that were baled up with it will sprout as well. Let it grow or pull it. It's up to you. You also may find that there was an occasional weed with a seed head within your bale, these can sprout, too. Pull them.

GREEN THUMB TIP: At the end of the season, you can use your straw to mulch trees and perennials for the winter. Just dry it out, first.

If landscape cloth or straw are out of your budget, you can also use your grass clippings. You can either mow your lawn, let them dry on your yard, then rake them up later. Or you can bag them as you cut. If you do bag them, spread them out on your driveway or patio to dry. If you have a tarred driveway, you're fortunate because they dry out quickly on a hot day! Just spread the clippings thinly and use a pitchfork or rake to fluff them in order to ensure they dry. Then take the dry clippings and begin to spread them in the rows of your garden. This is a very gradual way to cover your rows and fight weeds, but the clippings are free and will work their way into your soil.

> GREEN THUMB TIP: Do not use grass clippings from grass that has been treated for weed control or fertilized.

By staying ahead of the weeds in your garden, you are freeing up a lot of your summer for other things. You will be glad that you took the time and effort now as weeding can turn into a daunting chore if neglected or ignored. You'll even feel comfortable taking a vacation for a week or two knowing that they won't be too out of hand when you return.

> GREEN THUMB TIP: If you fish, save the heads and guts that you would normally discard after cleaning your catch. Instead of throwing them out, wrap them up tightly in plastic bag and store them in your deep freeze. Next Spring when you plant, you can put some in each hole that you dig for your transplants in place of fertilizer.

If you do plan a vacation or if you want to eliminate yet another task, purchase a timer for your soaker hoses. These work great! You can set them for the optimal time of day to water without having to remember to turn the faucet on and off. You can set them in sync with city water restrictions, and you don't need to ask your neighbor to do it for you. You can use them year after year if you give them proper care.

By mid-June, your beans will be impressing you with their size, they may even be reaching the top of the chicken wire tent. Soon, you'll want to remove any tents, however, try to wait until they establish their second set of leaves; it's the tenderness of the first set of leaves that seems to attract rabbits to beans. It has been my observation that rabbits tend to leave the beans alone once the second set of leaves have reached their full size. I also have never had a problem with rabbits and my dry beans. I do not even bother covering them. If you see the bean leaves working their way through the chicken wire, poke them back down to give them a little more time under this protective cover. You can also pull the chicken wire up, allowing it to hover above the beans by pulling the staples up an inch or so. But, eventually, the wire must be removed.

When it is time to remove the wire, which you can save and store for next year, prepare to give your beans support for the weeks to come.

Providing Support

Pound a sturdy stake at each end of the row so that you have at least 18 inches out of the ground. Take some untreated baler twine and tie it securely to a stake on one end and pull it so that it is directly above your row and tie it to the opposite stake so that it is taut. Tie as high up on the stake as you can. Along this tight twine, you will be tying each plant loosely with cotton string that runs from the lower part of the stalk straight up to the twine. As your bean grows, you can encourage it up and around its own trellis. Bush beans do not have tendrils so you will need to do this gently for each plant. It may sound like pesky work, but it is worth it. By the time your plant reaches the height of the twine, it will be well supported and off the ground. When your plants begin to flower and produce, your beans will grow straight and much easier to spot when picking.

GREEN THUMB TIP: You can use this support method for a variety of vegetables and flowers.

Toward the end of June, you can fertilize if you choose. Use a fertilizer that is specifically for vegetables. If you are using heirloom seeds, going the route of a homemade compost tea or organic manure is a good idea as your fertilizer could affect any seeds you intend to save.

July

Average MN High: 83° F

Average MN Low: 64° F

July is a busy month where everything seems to grow overnight. In addition, you probably have things such as picnics and vacations planned. This is where the automated watering, and mulching or covering the walkways between your garden rows pays off. These two steps allow you more freedom to leave your garden unattended without worries for days at a time.

If it turns out that Mother Nature has been or will be providing adequate rain, great! Just turn off your water. If you are leaving town and the forecast is predicting rain but you have some doubts, there are some automatic water timers which can be outfitted with a moisture sensor. Your water will then not come on unless it is required.

Tomatoes from my cherry tomato plants harvested in July!

Keeping Up

Beans are about the busiest vegetable in the garden, which is why they are often uses as an example in this book. If you got your beans planted on time, you will be picking them in July. If you took the time to tie them up, picking will be fairly quick and easy. Of course, the quick part depends upon how many rows you planted.

When you go to your garden to harvest, bring along a large enough basket or container that will hold your produce so that you don't find yourself leaving your work to get another container. Have with you a separated five-gallon bucket or something similar in which you can throw any weeds that you come across while picking your veggies.

Also, bring along some garden tools. Something you may consider getting is one of those bucket tool pouches that carpenters use. They are designed to fit over a five-gallon bucket so you can use the inside of the bucket and the pouches all around the outside. By keeping your pruners, cutters, shears, twine, stakes, mallet, knives, supports, etc...all together this way, you will save yourself much time. You won't be searching for a particular tool when you could be getting real work done.

Work up and down your garden rows in an

orderly fashion so that anytime you need to stop, it's easy to pick up where you left off. If you have long rows of beans, and you are stopping randomly within a row, simply pound a short stake in the ground to mark your stopping point.

Address each plant individually. Tend to any needs it may have. If you come across a broken stem, take out your snips and get rid of it so that it doesn't rot and invite disease. Don't just pull it off, as that may cause more damage.

Check to see if it needs additional support and provide it if necessary. For tomatoes, using the Velcro support tape works great. It's wide enough so that it won't cut into the stem or branch as the weight of the fruit increases, and it's reusable year after year!

Pick your vegetables at the peak of ripeness for the best flavor. If you are preserving them in any way, plan to do so within a day of picking.

Unless you have planted heirlooms from which you can save the seeds for your next planting season, pick and get rid of any produce, such as beans or cucumbers, which have grown beyond its ideal size. Do not leave it to continue to deplete the plant of energy and nutrients that could be going toward the other flowers and produce that are growing on that plant. Throw your overripe foods in your mulch pit instead.

Before leaving for an extended vacation, go through your garden and harvest everything that you are able. If you do not have time to preserve it, bring it along with you. If this is not an option, refrigerate it or give it away. There is no sense in letting it go to waste nor letting it over-ripen in the garden. When you return, you will likely have beans, cucumbers, and tomatoes to pick.

The beginning to mid-July is a good time to plant a fresh row of beans. Depending upon the variety, beans can be picked anywhere from 45 to 70 from sowing, so plant accordingly. Planting a second harvest of beans is worth it, especially if you preserve them.

Rid your garden of any inferior or diseased plants. It is not worth trying to nurse these back to health as you
could jeopardize the health of the rest of your garden.

As your melons and squash begin to form, tuck some straw underneath them to keep them off of the soil which can cause them to rot. I gently lift mine every so often, fluff up the straw and slightly reposition them. Just be careful not to damage the vine.

It may seem crazy, but even as early as July you can find great end of the season deals on garden tools and equipment. Starting now and throughout the rest of the year, take note of things you need, or just would like to have, that will help you out in the garden. Take the list with you when you are out and about so that you can refer to it if you come across a sale. Check in at your favorite garden centers frequently to see what is on clearance. Keep in mind that they offer more than just tools and supplies. You can also find great deals on things like gardening books, bird baths, and other garden accents. There are great finds at estate and garage sales, too!

August

Average MN High: 80° F

Average MN Low: 62° F

By August, you garden will be at its peak. It's actually the most productive month for the Minnesota vegetable gardener. Your tomatoes will be ripening like crazy, especially if they get some cooler nights.

Continue to harvest and maintain your plants as you did in July. Should you come across any plants that you deem "spent," you can cut back any dead or rotting leaves and throw them in the compost, or you can cut off the entire plant at the soil line and throw it in the compost. Do not pull the plant up (roots and all) as it may disturb neighboring plants. The roots will decay in your garden and be beneficial to the soil the following year.

Final fertilizing will be most beneficial for your plants in early August. Try to keep two to three weeks between applications. If you have a compost pile, churn it up good at the beginning of August while there are still plenty of warm days left. If it has dried out, sprinkle it with water and churn the moisture into it. You don't want it muddy, but it should be moist. In fact, if it has been a wet year, "fluffing" it with a pitchfork is a good way to keep it from being saturated. You are preparing your compost to spread over your garden at the end of the season.

You'll probably feel like you're spending most of your time indoors if you are preserving the bulk of your harvest. You don't need to wait for two or three days' worth of harvest so that you can put up jars and jars all at one time. Instead, try processing each day. Your produce will be preserved promptly and it won't seem like such a daunting chore. When you're done for the day, clean up your equipment but don't put it away. Leave your canner on the stove, ready for tomorrows processing.

Pay attention to any melons that you have planted for ripeness. While they may be large in size, it doesn't mean that they are ripe. Your nose will tell you if a melon is ripe or not. Also, the vine should easily pull away from the fruit.

You can safely leave your winter squash in the garden in August, but be sure to pick it before the first frost (which can be as early as mid-September.) Other vegetables that will be ready for harvest are onions, carrots, and dry beans. Although, you may want your carrots to increase in size, it's a good idea to pull samples and try them. If they taste great, then go ahead and harvest them, as leaving them in the ground to long will cause them to become woody and less desirable.

Pick your dry beans as they dry on the vine and spread them in a single layer on a newspaperlined baking sheet so that they dry out even more. Shelling dry beans and peas is indoor, winter work.

Store your dried beans in a dark, cool room in clean, dry canning jars. They make the most wonderful soups and chili!

September

Average MN High: 72° F

Average MN Low: 52° F

September, the end of the Minnesota gardening season. Some gardeners are sad to see it go and others welcome a few months away from dealing with the picking and canning. No matter which category you fall into, you can look forward to enjoying the rewards of your small daily efforts each night at the dinner table all winter long. A well-stocked vegetable room is a comforting sight. If you get snowed in for a spell, knowing that you won't starve should take some weight off of your shoulders!

The Final Harvest

Pickings of ripened vegetables are less in September. You may see quite a few green tomatoes on the vine. Perhaps they will turn red before first frost, perhaps not. Why take the chance? You can make a delicious green tomato relish that can be used on hotdogs, in salads, or any way that you use relish.

Or you can pick them and let them "ripen" using various methods. You can let them ripen on the counter top, pull the entire plant and hang it upside down, or enclose your tomatoes in a box or bag along with an apple or banana. Apples, pears, and bananas will naturally emit ethylene gas and trapping this gas in with your green tomatoes will turn them red. An apple will not go bad as quickly as a banana or pear. If you have an abundance of tomatoes, you can ripen them over the next month. In order not to have to used them up all at once, set a few out on your counter in the warmer temps and individually wrap rest and store them in a box or grocery bag in a cool vegetable room. Remove any stems prior to storing, as well as any dirt or debris. Store only firm, sound tomatoes. Keep a close eye on your tomatoes and throw any that develop rot or become too soft into your compost.

As they turn red, bring them to the table to enjoy. (The term *ripen* is used loosely because they really just turn red and soften. They don't always get the vine ripened taste, but they are better than those purchased in a store as most have been picked green and *ripened* using ethylene gas.)

Continue to pick your dry beans and keeping an eye on your melons, squash, and potatoes. Once your potato plants have died back, dig them up so that they don't begin to rot. Dig them on a dry sunny day and let them cure in the open air for a day or two before storing. Do not store bruised or damaged potatoes. Also, do not store them near apples. Potatoes release a harmless gas as they age. This gas makes apples spoil faster. On the other hand, apples give off their own ethylene gas, which may keep your potatoes from sprouting. I have never tested this theory; however, I would think that one or two apples should do the trick. I, personally, do not store fresh apples and potatoes in the same room.

When the vines on your winter squash begin to fade and yellow, you can pick them, leaving at least three inches of vine attached. Allow them to cure in the dry fall air for a few days so the shell hardens, then store them in a cool, dark vegetable room.

> *GREEN THUMB TIP:* Harvest all of your crops before first frost unless your seed packet instructs otherwise.

Take advantage of dry September days to clean up your garden. Any plants that you pull at this point should be set aside and not yet added to your mulch pit. If you used straw, gather it into a heap and fluff it with a pitch fork. Once it is nice and dry, you can use it in other areas of your yard to cover any perennials that you may have. You can work it into your garden soil as well, but if it doesn't break down you'll find that it will wrap itself around your tiller tines.

Gather any Velcro plant supports and stick them on top of one another for easy storage. You can use these in following years. Throw away the twine and strings that were used for supports, pull up your stakes, and row markers.

GREEN THUMB TIP: A five-gallon bucket can be used to hold your stakes and markers. If storing them outside, drill holes in the bottom of the bucket and prop it up on a couple blocks of wood so water doesn't accumulate and rot the ends. Otherwise, tuck them away in a corner of a shed or garage.

Once your garden has been cleared, pull up your soaker hoses, placing the landscape staples in a pot so that they are all in one place for the next season. A pot works wonderfully because it already has drainage holes.

Drain your hoses completely by laying them out on a downhill angle in your yard or driveway. If you do not have a sloped area to use, simply start at one end and hold it above your head. Allow any water trapped within the hose to drain downward. Walk along the hose slowly, keeping the water flowing out the opposite end. Lay your drained hoses out to allow them some time to dry. Gently coil them up, as not to kink them, and tie the coil in two to three spots with twine. You can now hang your hoses up out of the way until they are needed next year.

Finally, pull up your landscape fabric, placing the staples in your pot with the others. You may wish to first take an old broom and sweep off any dust and dirt. (Don't worry, your neighbors will get used to this sight!) With the staples removed, pull the cloth out onto your lawn or driveway and flip it over. Allow the back side to dry and then sweep off any dirt. You want your row coverings to be clean and dry before you fold them up for storage. These should be kept in a shed or garage where they will stay dry.

Provided the soil isn't too moist, you can work your bed over with a garden spade or tiller. If you opt to add your straw to your garden, turn over the soil first, then spread the dry straw in a thin layer over the top. Now you can work it in with a pitchfork or spade. When it's time to till in the spring, you won't have much of an issue with the straw wrapping around your tines, as it has had time to break down.

October

Average MN High: 58° F

Average MN Low: 40° F

The cool nights are back and the days are noticeably shorter. You look over your cleaned garden and begin to think ahead of next year's lay out. Your vegetable room is stocked with food that you grew and preserved yourself. What a satisfying feeling! By starting early, planning ahead, and being organized, you got the most out of your gardening season.

Choose one of the warmer October days to sit out in your garden with your pencil and notebook. Think back to this past season and make notes about what you liked and didn't like about it. Take some pictures to help you visualize your garden. Note what worked and didn't work. Sketch out a plan for next year, but be willing to change it, as by January you may decide to grow something different or new, such as celery.

Before the first snow, spread your compost over the top of your garden. If you didn't compost, spread some manure over it. As you rake leaves in the fall, you can rake them over your garden bed, as well. All of this organic matter will improve your soil. If you add leaves, spread them in thin layers at a time and work them into the soil lightly with a spade or pitchfork. The next time you rake, do the same thing. This keeps the leaves from blowing away and from matting together and molding.

Make sure that all of your garden tools are cleaned and put away. Winterize your tiller so you can be confident that it will start next spring. Continue to watch for year-end sales on garden equipment and supplies.

November

Average MN High: 41° F

Average MN Low: 26° F

Now that the bulk of your outdoor work is done, focus on the indoor work. You can shell and store your dried beans and peas if you have them. Throw the empty shells into your compost. Grind your herbs. Store all of your dry harvests such as these in clean canning jars. Include the name and year that you grew and harvested them on the label.

GREEN THUMB TIP: Homegrown herbs make great gifts for the cooks in your life! Put them in an attractive spice jar and label them.

You can now feel at ease that your garden is "put away" for the season. You can relax and enjoy the holidays. Take advantage of this down time to educate yourself. Perhaps you are interested in putting in some fruit trees or berry bushes. Read your garden books or get some from the library and learn everything that you can about anything you'd like to focus on for next year's season. It's fun to try at least one new and unusual plant each year.

December

Average MN High: 27° F

Average MN Low: 12° F

Think outside the zone! You may live in Zone 4, but with careful planning and creating the proper environment, you can experiment with fruits and vegetables that are natives in zones 5-10. For example, if you get an avocado pit to sprout, while it may not produce fruit, it still makes and interesting house plant and adds a great accent to your patio in the warm summer months.

Start thinking about other areas of your yard. Currants tolerate quite a bit of shade and make fantastic jelly and wine.

You can spruce up every niche by planting a variety of perennials and annuals that bloom from early spring into late fall. Adding tropical plants such as Elephant Ears, caladiums, and ferns in decorative pots tucked way here in there along a tree line or shady corner make an otherwise dull view pop!

Consider putting in trellises for grapevines or Morning Glories. The possibilities are endless and a lot of fun to plan out on paper.

Look for gardening clubs in your area that you can join. Nobody understands a gardener like another gardener! Before you realize it, January is back, the seed catalogs arrive, and it's time to get back to work! You will be grateful for all of the notes that you took last year and it's fun–and interesting–to compare how one year differs from the last. I try to record the morning temperature each day when I get up. I also note the precipitation, if any. I now have well over 40 years of such notes and from three different homes. I don't discard the old notes. While my zone may have changed from a 4 to a 3, and my soil is a different type, I still find valuable information and notes that I have made over the years to which I can refer in a moment's notice.

Happy Gardening!

–Nancy Ann

Cool Weather Crops

Beet
Broccoli
Brussels Sprouts
Cabbage
Carrot
Cauliflower
Celeriac
Chicory
Collard
Endive
Kale
Kohlrabi
Leek
Onion
Parsnip
Pea
Potato
Radish
Rutabaga
Spinach
Swiss Chard
Turnip

Warm Weather Crops

Bean
Celery
Corn
Cucumber
Eggplant
Ground Cherry
Melon
Okra
Pepper
Pumpkin
Squash
Sweet Potato
Tomato

Container Gardening

Nearly all vegetables can be grown in containers with success as long as you provide ample soil and have proper drainage. This is great for those who live in an apartment or a townhome if you have the sun working in your favor. Your container need not to be limited to a traditional pot.

Take a look in your basement and garage. If it will hold soil and drain water, you likely can plant in it. Avoid any containers that have once housed a toxic substance. Old buckets, wooden baskets, and even an old wheelbarrow can be converted easily into an attractive planting bed by drilling holes and lining it with landscape cloth. Get creative!

Perennials that Feed You

What could be more appealing than planting something once and then being able to harvest it year after year? Consider incorporating some of the following common perennials into your garden. These will provide you with delicious goodness that you'll look forward to for years to come.

Asparagus
Blueberries
Bush Cherry
Currants
Grapes
Hazelnuts
Horseradish
Raspberries
Rhubarb
Strawberries

A Note on Pest Control

Pests in the garden are always of concern. Squirrels love to sit high above in the tree, watch you plant, then scurry down to dig up your corn seeds. Rabbits love to nip off the first emerging shoots of lettuce and beans. Then there are the insects. The ones that I find the most annoying are the Japanese Beetles. I've tried the traps that you can hang from a shepherd's hook, and they work fabulously. However, it is my opinion that they attract more of the bugs to my garden than what would otherwise have come had I not hung one up at all. There are other ways to combat these pests.

Japanese Beetles

Spraying the with a mild mixture of liquid dish detergent and water makes them readily fall off of your plant, but I'm not sure if it actually kills them or not. *If you do this, do not use dish detergent that is anti-bacterial.* Hand picking them is not pleasant, but it is effective. What I usually do now is take a five-gallon bucket with about 2 inches of water in it, get it as close to the plant were the bugs are and shake them off into the bucket. Once they hit the water, they cannot fly out. This is faster and easier than hand picking them. Of course, some get away, but a lot of them fall into the bucket.

Before resorting to chemicals for pest control, always keep in mind the health of your plants and the food that you are going to be eating. Garden dust is effective, but be sure to read the instructions thoroughly and take note of the days until it is safe to harvest.

Above are some of the most effective pest controllers that I use year after year. Mallard ducks. I buy them in the spring as 2 day old ducklings and they fly away in the fall.

Notes

Wish List

Other books by Nancy Ann

Home Fire: Sarah and Charlie

Home Fire: The Journey Home

Home Fire: The Big Year

www.nancyannbooks.com

Made in the USA
San Bernardino, CA
12 July 2017